# At the Doctor

Roderick Hunt • Annemarie Young
Alex Brychta

6

The children were excited. Miss
Green was telling them about a visit
to the zoo. They were going at the
end of the week.

She showed them a picture of two
tigers. "The zoo saved these tigers
from the hunters," said Miss Green.
"Let's find out about tigers."

Sam and Anna went to look at the
tiger books on the table.

"Come on Kipper," said Sam.
"Help us find a good one."

But Kipper didn't feel well. He
sneezed. He felt hot and he had a
runny nose. His throat was sore and
his head ached.

Anna went to Miss Green. "Kipper is crying," she said.

"He doesn't feel well," said Sam.

Miss Green felt Kipper's head.
"You do feel hot, Kipper. I think you
should go home. I'm going to call
your mummy."

Mum came to take Kipper home.
Kipper was upset. He didn't want to
be ill. He wanted to see the tigers at
the zoo.

"I think we should go and see my
friend Aza. She's a nurse at the
Health Centre," said Mum. "We'll go
on the way home."

Aza looked at Kipper's throat and then took his temperature.

"My ear hurts a bit, too," said Kipper.

"Keep him at home," said Aza.
"Give him lots to drink. Come back
if his ear ache gets worse."

Mum let Kipper lie on the sofa.
She gave him a book about tigers.
"I want to see the tigers at the
zoo," said Kipper.

That night, Kipper woke up. "My
ear really hurts," he said, "and
there's stuff coming out of it."

Dad gave Kipper some medicine.

The next day, Kipper felt worse.
"We'd better go and see the
doctor," said Dad. "The nurse told us
to go back if your ear got worse."

Kipper and Dad waited for the
doctor to call them.

"You'll like Dr Spooner," said Dad.
"She's really kind."

Dr Spooner listened to Kipper's
chest and took his temperature.
Then she looked in his ears.

"Poor Kipper," said Dr Spooner.
"You've got an ear infection. I'll give
you some ear drops and some
medicine to take."

"I want to see the tigers with my class tomorrow," said Kipper.

"I'm sorry," said Dr Spooner. "You have to wait until your ear is better."

By Sunday, Kipper felt a lot
better. His ear had stopped aching,
but he was sad that he had missed
the trip to see the tigers.

Sam came to see Kipper with Wilf
and Wilma. Sam was their cousin.

"I hurt my arm," said Sam, "so I
didn't see the tigers, either."

Just then, Mum came in. "We've got a surprise for you," she said.

Mum and Dad took them all to
the zoo!

"The tigers are fantastic,"
said Kipper.

"They're so big," said Sam.
"What's that tiger doing?"
asked Kipper.

"The tiger sneezed!" laughed Sam.
"I think it has a cold."

"I hope it doesn't have an
ear ache too!" said Kipper.

## Talk about the story

Why was Kipper upset at school?

What did Dr Spooner tell Kipper?

Why did Mum and Dad take the children to the zoo?

What makes you feel better when you are ill?

# What do you find at the doctor?

Talk about the things you see on this page. Can you think of anything else you might find at the doctor?

Now look back at the story and find these things in the pictures.

## The doctor uses these things to ...

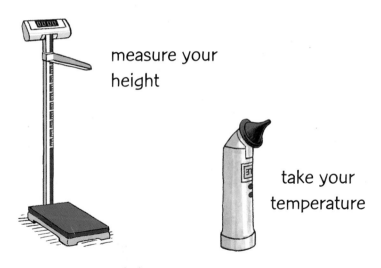

measure your
height

take your
temperature

measure your weight

check your eyes

check your
ears

listen to your chest and heart

look inside your
mouth

# Spot the difference

Find the five differences in the two tiger cubs.